GIVENDALE

GIVENDALE

A Farm in Harmony with Nature

Richard Fuller ARPS

SWAN HILL
PRESS

DEDICATION

To my wife Frances in appreciation of all the hours I have spent 'gone missing' with my camera and to our two sons, David and Robert, whose help in locating subjects and building hides has been invaluable.

Copyright © 1991 by Richard Fuller

First published in the UK in 1991 by
Swan Hill Press
An Imprint of Airlife Publishing Ltd.

British Library Cataloguing in Publication Data
Fuller, Richard
Givendale : a farm in harmony with nature
1. Great Britain. Agriculture
I. Title
338.10941

ISBN 1 85310 230 X

Printed by Kyodo Printing Co. (S'pore) Pte Ltd., Singapore.

Swan Hill Press

An Imprint of Airlife Publishing Ltd.
101 Longden Road, Shrewsbury SY3 9EB, England.

CONTENTS

A pair of green woodpeckers rear their young every year in a freshly bored hole, usually in an old ash tree. The farm provides ideal habitat for their food source — insects in the bark of trees and on the ground old pastures and woodlands which are rich in ants and various larvae. The nesting site of this elusive bird is difficult to find and it wasn't until May 1991 that I found one, forty feet up in an ash tree. I constructed a hide bit by bit until it was finally complete just eight feet away from the nest hole. From this position, high in the trees, I enjoyed watching and photographing the comings and goings of these spectacular birds until one evening in early July the first fledgling to leave the nest emerged. Calling frantically to her attendant father, the speckled youngster climbed unsurely up the tree on very wobbly legs. The next day the whole brood had left.

Opposite: A brimstone butterfly feeds on the flower of a sow thistle growing on undisturbed land adjacent to a farm track.

*The author, with his sister Rosemary, in a hay field at Hendy Farm,
with waggoner Di Evans and one of the farm's Shire horses.*

INTRODUCTION

The ways of the countryside have played a major part in my life from a very early age.

My father was involved with manufacturing aircraft, and during the war he was posted to North Wales, where the production of aircraft parts continued under the protection of the deep slate quarries. And so in 1943 I was born in a tiny village in Snowdonia, and when I was about two years old we moved to an old lodge on the outskirts of Caernarfon.

Surrounded by woods and fields, and much to my mother's consternation, I started to wander further and further from home, and soon I came across the man whose influence was to shape the rest of my life. Mr Jones from Hendy Farm was a bachelor who lived with his sister, and together they farmed about 250 acres. I gradually spent more and more time with Mr Jones — he was a kind and gentle man. During the school holidays and at weekends he would pick me up from home at about 6.30 am in his little old Morris truck, and we would look round his cattle which grazed the fields near our home. Then we would drive back to the farm and, after doing various jobs, we would go into the big farmhouse kitchen for breakfast. In those days lots of men were employed on the farm to look after the teams of big shire horses, and to do much of the work which is now done by machines. The men would come into the kitchen and sit down round a long, scrubbed table and help themselves to porridge out of a huge pan. They covered thick slices of bread with home-made butter and fat pork.

At the age of five or six I found such a gathering rather awesome, but gradually I got used to their teasing ways, just as I did to the great stag turkey which regularly chased me across the farmyard.

I have many memories of those early days at Hendy. There were not many tractors yet in that area and I can still picture the magnificent white shire stallion that was taken round to neighbouring farms to serve the mares. Those were the days of horse-drawn binders, and the sheaves of wheat and oats were brought home by horses and carts to be stacked in the huge red barn, in preparation for threshing during the winter.

Threshing days were always exciting. The great machines were driven by steam engines, and frenzied activity would fill the stackyard. The pulleys on the threshing machine and the big baler whizzed round and round driven by huge flat belts, with dust and smoke filling the air. Each of the dozen men had his own specific job to do, and when I grew older and stronger I was promoted to wheeling the bags of grain from the threshing machine across the yard to the sack hoist which lifted the sacks up into the granary to be stored. My pay for the day was as much wheat as I could carry the mile home across the fields to feed my chickens. The highlight for me came at the end of threshing when the whole stackyard was encircled with wire netting so that all the rats that were living in the stack were prevented from escaping. As the stack dwindled to the last layer or two of sheaves the farm's corgis rushed round snapping at the rats as they tried to make their escape.

Sometimes there were so many rats that men armed with pitch-forks had to give a helping hand. We all made sure our trousers' bottoms were tied with string at the ankle!

I learned quickly that life in the countryside was often associated with death. Rabbits and pigeons were shot because they damaged the crops, and also because they were a good source of food in those post-war years of rationing. Carrion crows and foxes were regarded as enemies of the farmer's flocks, so they were destroyed whenever possible. My shooting trips with Mr Jones influenced my development as a keen sportsman in a way which then seemed inextricably part of my fascination for wildlife.

Around the farmyard, nature used to take its course more often than it does today. Modern drugs alleviate much of the animals' suffering that went on in those days before the advent of antibiotics and anthelmintics. I vividly remember some sad occasions when animals died after exhaustive treatments with ineffective therapies.

My walks home from Hendy across the fields brought me into close contact with my natural surroundings. The thick hedges and the stone walls provided habitats for all sorts of animals and plants. Sometimes I would make a detour through two spinneys to see what I could find, and each had its own attractions. In one of them, high up in the trees, herons nested. These huge grey birds fascinated me, and I used to collect the hatched blue egg-shells from under the nests. In the other spinney there was a marshy area and a pond, and in the spring the king-cups formed a spectacular canopy under which the clear water teemed with frogs and newts, performing their extraordinary mating rituals.

Gradually I became more involved with farm life at Hendy and my interest in wild creatures became so intense that my school work suffered, and my parents despaired whenever they read my school reports, but Mr Jones continued to guide and teach me. He took me to market on many occasions, and he taught me to drive his little old Morris truck and even the new Fordson tractor. Above all, he managed over the years to instill in me an irrepressible feeling for the farm animals, for the land and for the countryside. By the time I was about eight years old I had made the decision to be a farmer. Accepting the situation, my mother bought me two books, both of which I worshipped. One was the *Observer Book of British Birds* and the other one was about

farming entitled *Both Sides of the Road*, beautifully illustrated by Charles Tunnicliffe.

In 1954, when I was eleven years old, we moved to Shropshire. My father had softened the blow by describing the big modern farms and by telling me that the opportunities were better; but before we left we bought a cottage in the village where I had been born, and we were to spend many happy holidays there and I kept in touch with Mr Jones until he died.

My father had managed to find us a house in a hamlet near the village of Nesscliffe. To my delight my bedroom window overlooked the farmyard, where I was to spend much of my time developing my ambition to be a farmer. The area around our house appeared to me like Paradise. Our large garden led down to a small copse of mature trees under which thick bushes concealed many birds' nests in the spring. Across the fields several ponds had their own attractions for me; the moorhens, the mallard and the frogs fascinated me. The thick hedges which linked several spinneys provided an abundant supply of berries for the visiting redwings, and in one of the spinneys a tawny owl nested every year in a hollow elm tree. Nesting birds had a special appeal for me, and I used to spend much of my time in the spring hunting for their nests and eggs. I built up a collection of over a hundred different species before the days of legal protection.

I continued to find school work difficult, and my outdoor pursuits made getting down to homework a tedious chore. My interest in shooting continued to grow, so my father bought me a shotgun for my sixteenth birthday. Shooting has given me an enormous amount of pleasure over the years, and has been very much a part of my wildlife interests.

That may sound strange, but man has evolved as a predator and the basic instincts of manipulating our surrounding resources for our own needs seemed to be fairly strong in my personal make-up.

I was also keen to learn more about my quarry so I built large aviaries and kept pheasants and waterfowl. I collected their eggs and hatched them under my bantams. I also had an aviary in which I kept homing pigeons. I used to test their 'homing' ability by letting them go out of the window of the school bus. I remember that my favourite pigeon was jet black with white wing-tips.

I continued to spend much of my spare time helping on the farm. I enjoyed working with the cows, and as I grew older I helped to cultivate the land and to harvest the crops.

I eventually managed to pass four 'O' level exams at school which assured me a place at Harper Adams Agricultural College. I duly embarked on the National Diploma in Agriculture course which in those days was intensely academic. I found it hard going and I longed to be back working on the land. I failed my first year exams, and that ended my academic career.

My first full-time job was milking one hundred Friesian cows on the farm back home, for which I was paid £7 a week for seventy-two hours work. I immersed myself in my work because I was determined to make my career as a farm manager. I realised that it was a difficult way forward as competition for the good jobs was intense, and my failure at college meant that my practical skills would have to compensate for my academic shortcomings.

After nearly two years of milking cows I realised that I had to broaden my experience, so I obtained a job on a large arable farm in Oxfordshire. My duties included rearing pheasants for the farm shoot, and so my hobby had suddenly become part of my job. I was able to study the wildlife on the farm and actually get paid for it. After about a year I was approached by an old college friend, Peter Diment, to set up a dairy herd for the farmer he worked for. I saw this as a useful step up my career ladder and so I accepted. My previous experience with dairy cows stood me in good stead and I spent about two years developing an eighty-cow herd of Ayrshires.

Peter and I had kept in touch with each other since leaving college. We shared the same sporting interests, and we had a lot of fun travelling to different places on shooting expeditions, from wild goose shooting on the Solway Firth to rough shooting in the Scottish Borders and to Dorset, Peter's home county.

It was while I was working with Peter that I met my future wife. Frances was a student at a teacher training college near Oxford. We met in a pub one evening, and we were married just over a year later. Shortly after our marriage I was successful in gaining my first job as a farm manager running a 250-acre farm in the Chiltern Hills. We were to spend four years at Ashridge Farm during which time our two sons were born. My meagre salary of about £75 a month left little for luxuries although I did manage to run a car. I was able to help with the housekeeping by growing vegetables, by keeping poultry for eggs and meat and by shooting rabbits and pigeons for the pot. We also kept a Jersey cow for our milk supply and I reared calves in a redundant farm building to earn extra cash. The hours were long and the work was hard but youthful strength and my determination to better myself carried us through what were difficult but happy times.

The break-up of my employer's marriage brought our time at Ashridge to an end. The farm was to be sold and I had to find another job. After several interviews I was offered a job managing High Belthorpe, a 450-acre farm in East Yorkshire. At the time I had no idea that my acceptance of that job was to lead us, within eighteeen months, just up the hill to Givendale.

There is little room for sentiment in today's technological age when running a successful farming business, but there is room to share the countryside with a wide variety of flora and fauna.

In recent years the industry has been encouraged by government policies to intensify production systems and to bring into cultivation many areas of land hitherto untouched. These central strategies have in fact ensured that the population has wanted for nothing but the price has been high as many species of wildlife have been squeezed into smaller and smaller corners of suitable habitat. However, farmers and their masters are not solely responsible for the erosion of our wild places, commerce too has played a significant role, with its obsession for expansion and profit. Urban development has swallowed up huge areas of land, so too have many hundreds of miles of motorways as they carve huge swathes through the countryside ignoring ancient badger setts or old meadows rich in wild flowers.

We all indulge ourselves in our modern materialistic society, all too ready to blame someone else for our deteriorating environment, frequently encouraged by the media determined to create sensational stories, often far removed from the facts.

Contrary to popular belief, the majority of farmers like myself care a great deal about the environment in which they live and work.

Experience has taught us to respect the harsh realities of the changing seasons and to take nothing for granted. Traditionally we have responded positively to change but we have always strongly defended our livelihoods and the resources from which they are gained.

Change is on the way again as European Community strategists encourage farmers to move towards the intensification of 'environmentally friendly' production systems. British farmers will again respond positively and will be happy to do so providing that they are able to stay in business but the central planners are ultimately responsible for feeding us all. It is to be hoped that their new policies don't underfeed us by as much as their old ones overfed us. It is all too easy to be complacent in times of plenty.

Young ash, field maple, crab apple, wild cherry and oak trees have been planted out on the grassland, carefully following the contours of the ground and protected from the livestock by strong wooden guards.

GIVENDALE

The conscientious way in which I had approached my work over the years had at last paid off. I was appointed farm manager by a very progressive farming company to run their newly acquired 1000-acre Givendale Farm. So on 10 October 1974 I started what has been for me an immensely enjoyable and rewarding way of life.

The farm needed to be brought up to date and it was made clear to me that the unit had to be managed on productive and profitable lines to justify the large capital investment. Part of the original management plan for the farm read as follows: 'The achievement of the targets and returns which are required to justify the capital investment in the farm will be achieved only if the problem of rabbit infestation, lack of stock fencing, scrub clearance and permanent pasture improvement can be overcome in the first eighteen months. There is no reason why more efficient farming should detract from the amenity aspects of the land. In fact, improvements in terms of access, woodland and pond landscaping will enhance both the sporting and wildlife preservation considerations, which can go hand in hand with productive farming.'

So we set about re-modelling an area of land which had tremendous potential for the successful integration of productive farming with a healthy wildlife environment. The topographical features of Givendale with 300 acres of steep permanent grassland, 700 acres of arable crops, 50 acres of scattered, small, mature woods linked by good hedges, and, above all, the presence of two spring-fed streams provided an ideal network of habitat to support a balanced and varied wildlife population.

While planning the new layout of the farm I was very conscious not only of ways of improving its efficiency and productivity, but also of ways of improving the existing wildlife habitat and preserving the natural features of the landscape. Areas of scrub-land had to be cleared so that we could develop profitable beef and sheep enterprises, but in the process quite large areas of rough grass and thickets were preserved by fencing them off. These areas have since proved valuable because they provide habitats for small rodents to support barn owls and kestrels. Probably the most rewarding single project I undertook was the creation of four large ponds. The presence of water in an area not only enriches the variety of wildlife to be found there but also adds immensely to the visual attractiveness of the landscape.

The ponds were created by damming the streams and they lie naturally in the flat bottom of the valley. The marshy margins surrounding the ponds have been fenced off to protect the plants from cattle and sheep grazing. While constructing the ponds I paid particular attention to creating varying depths of water to accommodate different species of plants and animals. For instance, the spotted orchids and the marsh valarian grow in the damp margins while buckbean and reedmace actually grow in the water. Wading birds such as the common sandpiper like to hunt for shrimps on the shingle at the very edge of the water while dabbling ducks such as mallard and teal feed in the shallows. Deeper water provides the hunting grounds for diving birds such as the tufted duck, the dab-chick or a visiting goldeneye.

I have paid attention to the woodland margins by keeping them cut back, to allow shrubs and wild flowers to flourish. The roadside verges are mown only once a year during the winter. This practice has encouraged a healthy wild flower population, which also supports large numbers of butterflies.

The area of woodland has been increased by planting two two-acre areas of arable land with larch, beech and sycamore, and numerous ash and field maple trees have been planted on the permanent grassland.

13

Of course one could do more, but a balance has to be struck between the preservation of habitat and earning a living from the land. The skill in combining the two is to recognise the opportunities and then to manage them together in the most effective way.

This book is essentially a means of sharing my photography with a wider audience, but it is not just a wildlife album. Above all, I am a farmer and my fascination for wildlife is very much part and parcel of that. My farming objectives with respect to efficient productivity are complemented but not compromised by my conservation objectives. This is no limp 'green solution': It is a strong brown one. This is my bit of the Yorkshire countryside and what follows sets out my view of my life's work on it.

A stream of pure spring water encircles an alder tree; at its base growing in the slack water, yellow flag and butterbur leaves cast their shadows and the golden flowers of the marsh marigold add a splash of colour to the burgeoning scene.

The ancient woodland provides a wealth of habitat for many species of plants, insects, birds and animals.

Over the years I have encouraged the thorn hedges to grow higher and wider to provide thick cover for nesting song birds and abundant berries for them to feed on during the winter. At ground level the wide base provides ideal habitat for species of small rodents and cover for nesting game birds. These important wildlife corridors are protected from crop sprays by leaving a strip of bare ground between the crop and the hedge bottom. In return the crops are protected from invading weeds and undesirable grasses.

WINTER

There are plenty of jobs to be done on the farm during the early weeks of winter. The stock sheds have to be made ready as groups of cattle are gradually brought inside. The shepherd weighs the lambs each week to find the ones heavy enough to sell, and he is mindful that tupping time is approaching. The ewes must be in good condition when the rams are turned in, so a period of flushing on good quality grass ensures optimum ovulation for twin embryos to be implanted. The shepherd splits the ewes into flocks of about 200 so that six rams can work in each. On 15 November, the raddle harnesses are strapped onto the rams and they are turned in with the ewes. Fixed to the harnesses are blue crayons so when the ewes are served they are left with blue marks on their rumps. After about ten days the colour is changed to red. This colour coding of the ewes tells the shepherd exactly when to expect them to lamb the following April so he is able to pen them in appropriate groups in the lambing sheds.

Back at the farmyard the arable staff are busy in the grain store loading lorries with 450 tonnes of wheat. Usually it is sold to be fed to pigs, but if the quality is good enough then it is used for biscuit making by one of the national millers.

By the end of November all the cattle have been housed and they settle down on diets of silage, straw and cereals. The rations vary to fit the requirements of each class of stock and they are designed to maintain economic performance of the animals. Those which are young and still growing or lactating need a higher plane of nutrition than mature dry cows. At this time of year I am aware that the energy requirement of the suckling cows is at its highest because calf demand for milk is at its peak and they are trying to prepare their reproductive systems for re-breeding. So to achieve satisfactory reproductive performance the cows are fed a high plane of nutrition up to and during the mating period. Our three stock bulls are turned out, one into each yard, on 3 December and they stay with the cows for six weeks by which time the cows will be back in calf. The stockman keeps a close eye on the bulls to make sure they continue to work properly and he records each mating to form the basis of our progeny testing procedure.

Work with the cattle takes up much of the daylight hours but there is also time for jobs that have been put off through pressure of work. On fine days, outside tasks such as building repairs or re-hanging a damaged field gate all add to the variety of the work. On grey, wet days workshop jobs may include building a new calf feeder or repairing a bent straw rack.

During the winter months farmers around the country hold meetings to discuss wide ranging topics associated with the industry. These meetings are either formal conferences held on a national scale, or more frequently they are informal discussions between local groups of farmers. I attend several each winter, either as a member of the audience or in many cases as a speaker on beef production and to a lesser extent on the conservation of wildlife in the context of agriculture. I give most of my talks in Yorkshire but I have also travelled as far afield as Cambridge, Dorset and Cheshire, the Isle of Arran and Orkney. I enjoy these trips immensely, not only because I meet many interesting people but also because it gives me the chance to see new countryside and, hopefully, some of its wildlife.

For similar reasons I also enjoy a day's game shooting with friends. Winter field sports are very much part of the farming scene. There is of course the skill of being able to shoot well and work a gun dog effectively, but in addition they

Opposite: A fresh fall of snow clings to the branches before it soon crashes to the ground in wet lumps, warmed by the weak rays of the sun.

are social occasions when friends can meet on each other's farms away from the pressures of work. Sportsmen have over the years contributed significantly towards habitat and wildlife preservation. In years gone by large estate owners laid out their land with pheasant shooting as their top priority. Many of our marvellous mature woodlands were planted by them to show their pheasants to the Guns in the most spectacular way.

Unfortunately, the game keepers of those days did everything in their power to exterminate so-called 'vermin' such as all species of birds of prey, badgers, hedgehogs etc. Fortunately, today's keepers are more enlightened, and their methods of managing shoots have great benefits for the wildlife population as a whole. For instance, the planting of new woodland or temporary pheasant cover such as kale or canary grass provides ideal habitat and winter feeding for a variety of wildlife. Digging ponds for duck shooting also creates a whole new habitat, and many species of small birds survive the hard winter months by sharing food put out for pheasants and ducks.

The beneficial effects of sporting activities are not readily understood by many people who frown disapprovingly at these 'barbaric' pastimes. In reality, many species of birds and animals have longer and fitter lives, while woodland glades abound with wild flowers and ponds teem with life. In the vast majority of cases these wildlife havens have been created by sporting landowners and farmers who understand the real ways of the countryside.

Routine work with the livestock dominates the short winter days, although when weather permits, outside jobs such as fencing repairs are a welcome change. In the farm workshop, machinery maintenance is very important to ensure that the machines are ready for work when they are needed later in the year.

Snowfalls are common and usually create a considerable amount of extra work. The exposed situation of the farm means that snow blows into the stock sheds and the steep roads leading up to the farm very quickly fill with drifting snow.

That is when the big four-wheel drive tractor is hitched up to the snowplough and goes roaring away down the road with snow flying off the huge blades. With the low temperature come the problems of frozen pipes and water troughs. The daily thawing-out process with hot water is time-consuming but essential to keep the stock watered.

When the first snow falls it is time to bring the 650 mule ewes into their winter quarters. Housing the ewes during the winter in groups of forty is desirable because they can be fed and looked after efficiently in a controlled environment. If they were left outside then situations such as severe weather or inadequate feeding could lead to stress-related diseases and poorer breeding performance.

The ewes are fed on home-produced wheat straw that has been treated with anhydrous ammonia. This treatment improves the feeding value of the straw by breaking down the lignin in it, which increases the digestibility of the straw. This is a fairly new technique and it is highly desirable because it economically produces improved feeding material from poor quality straw and it eliminates the need to burn it in the fields at harvest time.

In the cattle sheds the stockman and his assistant spend their time carting feed and bedding the yards with straw. The breeding herd of 150 Angus x Friesian suckler cows is split into two groups. Eighty of them calve in September and October while the other seventy calve in February and March. These cross-bred cows are mated to pure Charolais bulls and the resulting calves are suckled by their mothers for seven to ten months before being fattened for good quality beef.

Breeding good quality cattle is very satisfying, but it can only be achieved by continually paying careful attention to strict management standards. A close watch is kept on the cows and calves for signs of disease, and it is important to make sure that they are fed at a level which will support economic performance.

Out in the fields the crops that were sown in the autumn often lie under a layer of snow which gives protection from the cold winds and frosts. Only the oil seed rape plants may poke through the snow, inviting huge flocks of wood-pigeons for a feed. Thousands of pigeons migrate from Scandinavia each winter to swell our native population, and unless they are deterred from landing in the rape fields they will cause considerable damage. Scarecrows and bangers are used to try to move them on, and regular patrols are necessary to ensure that these measures are working.

Right: A year's growth of a hawthorn hedge that we planted is highlighted in a rain storm.

Below: A thin film of ice covers the ponds as the first sharp frost reminds us of the approaching winter.

'Gold Leaf.' The skeleton of a poplar leaf.

Milk caps caught against a brilliant blue sky.

The shepherd weighs and selects lambs for market. He is looking for those which are a good weight but not too fat.

Bonnet mycena growing in semi-darkness under a thick canopy of dense fir trees.

Sycamore fruits ready to spin to earth on gossamer wings.

Opposite: One of our Charolais bulls, aptly named Tarzan on account of his huge size.

Below: The long-lasting berries of black bryony add colour to the otherwise drab hedgerows.

Opposite: Hoar frost has formed on this nettle leaf.

A pheasant's footprints moulded in the frozen snow.

The subtle colours of the bracket fungus Imomotus radiatus *enhance the north facing side of an alder tree.*

Winter in Givendale. The thirteenth-century church stands in a small copse of sycamore and horse-chestnut trees overlooking the ponds and the woodland of Givendale valley. The fabric of this attractive, peaceful church has deteriorated over the years and the village people have been raising funds to repair the roof. My contribution has been to present shows of my wildlife slides to public audiences.

Icicles form near the splashing water of a stream.

Velvetshank lit by the pale winter sunshine while being frozen solid. This is one of the few varieties of gill-bearing fungi to be found in the winter.

The setting sun picks out frozen snow drifts on a road leading up to the farm.

A spider's web is slung between two dead willow-herb plants in readiness to capture flying insects, even during the depth of winter.

The shepherd moves a flock of ewes to more sheltered ground after a heavy snowfall.

SPRING

The suckler cows start to calve at the beginning of February and continue until the end of March. They are housed in yards which are well bedded with plenty of warm straw, and careful stockmanship is maintained to ensure that the calves are delivered safely. The majority of the cows calve quite normally without interference, but it is never possible to predict which cow is likely to need assistance and so a constant watch is kept on the herd during this period. Once a cow has started to calve then the experienced stockman knows if she needs help to deliver her calf safely. It may, for example, be mal-presented or just too big to be born naturally. Every effort is made to ensure that each cow has a live calf. A dead calf is not only a tragic waste of its nine-month gestation period but it is also a financial loss to the farm.

As soon as a calf is born its mother licks it dry. This stimulates it and helps to form a bond between them. The calf is soon on its feet and suckling the vital colostrum in the first milk from its mother's udder. A calf is born without any antibodies to protect it from bacterial infections. These antibodies are carried in the cow's colostrum so the early absorption by the calf of a sufficient quantity is vital for its survival.

The attention I have paid to developing management techniques for the herd has been rewarded by significant improvements in performance. For example, the calf weaning weight increased by 30 per cent between 1978 and 1987. The results I have achieved were recognised in 1983 when Givendale was awarded a 'Grass to Meat' Award by the Meat and Livestock Commission and the British Grassland Society. Since then it has given me great pleasure to host farm visits showing beef producers from all parts of the country how I tackle the task of making money out of suckled calf production. I am also invited to give illustrated talks to groups of farmers at their winter meetings.

In addition to the Angus x Friesian cows there are about forty pedigree Charolais cows on the farm, which also start to calve in February. These cows are kept to breed pure Charolais bulls for use as crossing sires to produce beef calves from cross-bred cows. Some of these bulls we keep for our own use, but the majority are sold to other breeders. Detailed recording of the herd helps to identify animals which have superior conformation and natural growth potential, and this information is used in planned herd improvement. The Charolais breed originates from France and it is renowned for breeding fast growing cattle which reach heavy weights and produce lean meat.

I like to leave a field of corn stubble over the winter as a source of food for the grey partridges and small birds such as finches. When the weather permits it must be ploughed during February so that the furrows have time to weather before the next crop of spring barley is sown. Towards the end of the month the autumn-sown crops of barley, wheat and oil seed rape gradually start to turn greener. Growth is slow at this time of the year and the winter rain and snow have depleted the nutrients in the soil. As a result, it will soon be time for us to feed the crops with fertiliser.

March is often a cold, wet month as raw winds blow from the north-east bringing with them heavy showers of sleet and rain inland from a grey North Sea. The rare spells of brighter weather are very welcome because, despite the chill in the air, the crops are beginning to grow in response to the lengthening days, and it is time for us to be out on the land.

Early in the month the first of three applications of fertiliser is applied to the crops and to

Opposite: The brilliant golden flowers and bright green, glossy leaves of the marsh-marigold are a magnificent sight as they grow on the edges of the springs, streams and ponds.

33

the grassland. Nitrogen fertiliser is an essential part of crop husbandry; without it yields would be very low, farming would be uneconomical, and there would be serious shortages of grain, meat and milk. The careful management of split applications of fertiliser reduces the risk of nitrates leaching from the soil and they also feed the plants regularly as they grow. The accurate application of the fertiliser is important, so the spreading machine must be well maintained and it must be precisely calibrated. In addition, to ensure that even spreading is achieved 'tramlines' are made in the crop by blocking off some of the drill spouts at sowing time to create measured lines in the crop for the tractor and spreader to follow. The first application of fertiliser is small to match the slow growth of the plants in early March.

Grass is a very important crop at Givendale, with nearly half the farm growing various types of it to feed all the livestock. There are many varieties of grass which have been bred by plant breeders to do different jobs; some persist longer than others, some are more frost-resistant than others, some are more suited to grazing than to mowing. Then there are some wild grasses which are serious weeds in the corn crops, such as sterile brome and couch-grass.

There are three types of grass mixtures which are grown on the farm, all of which contribute in different ways to feeding the cattle and the sheep. The most productive of them are the short-term rye-grass leys which are grown for two years as cereal break crops in the arable rotation. These leys are divided into two types. One is a mixture of tall, high yielding grasses which is used for making into silage to feed the cattle during the winter. The other mixture has clover in it and forms a dense sward close to the ground, and it is used for grazing some of the sheep. The third type is old, permanent grazing pasture which consists of indigenous varieties of rye grasses, cocksfoot and clover. These areas are not quite so productive but improvement has been achieved by using fertilisers and by controlling the grazing density of the livestock on them. These measures have had the effect of encouraging the more

vigorous varieties of grass in the sward to flourish. This has resulted in higher stocking rates, but to ensure that there is enough grass at the end of April to feed 200 cows and their calves, and 620 ewes with their 1200 lambs, it is essential to apply the fertiliser in early March. This in itself can be difficult because the steep grassland is usually wet at this time of year making it dangerous to drive on, even with a four-wheel drive tractor. Sometimes, therefore, the fertiliser is spread from an aeroplane.

While all the activity is going on in the fields, life is still busy in the stock sheds. The cows are still calving and they continue to demand close attention. The young calves are susceptible to digestive and respiratory diseases so they must be watched carefully so that at the first signs of trouble, they can be treated with the appropriate drugs. In the sheep sheds the shepherd is mindful that lambing is due to start soon, so he prepares his lambing equipment. The daily feeding routine continues with a close eye on the forage stocks; although careful budgeting should see us through the winter, we don't want to run short.

As the days lengthen and the temperature gradually rises so the warming soil triggers an acceleration in the growth of grass and corn. Early April is usually the time for sowing spring barley. I hope for a spell of dry weather so that the seed beds for the new crop can be prepared. The two fields of barley are grown as seed crops — that is to say the crop is sold as seed stock for other farmers to plant. This means that I have to take extra care in growing these crops to make sure that it is not contaminated by weed seeds.

The rapidly growing crops soon require feeding again, so the third and final application of nitrogen fertiliser is applied to the winter corn and to the silage leys. Quite often in April strong winds and heavy showers hamper field work and so it can be frustrating trying to get all the work done on time. This is particularly the case when it comes to spraying the crops to protect them from harmful fungal diseases.

The ewes which are still in their straw-bedded yards are looking wider, their udders are starting to show signs of freshening, and soon the first lambs will be born. Lambing is due to start in the middle of the month but some lambs will be born earlier. The shepherd watches his sheep with growing attention. With 620 ewes to lamb in just three weeks the lambing operation is a very busy time, so he is joined by an assistant and they share shifts which ensures twenty-four hour observation.

The shepherd hopes to turn each ewe away with two lambs, but he knows that to achieve that he must literally live with his sheep and employ all the management skills that he has developed over the years. As the ewes lamb they are put in individual pens and they stay in them for about two days. This period of close proximity helps to form the bond between the mother and her lambs which will keep them together as a family unit until the lambs are weaned in August. When the ewes and their lambs are taken out of the individual pens they are put into groups of about twenty. The lambs grow quickly and by the time they are about a week old they are then strong enough to be turned out into the fields. This can be a worrying time for the shepherd because heavy rain and cold winds can result in lambs dying from hypothermia, so a close watch is kept on the weather forecast for signs of inclement conditions. Once they are turned out into fresh nutritious grass the ewes milk very well and their lambs grow rapidly. There is no better sight for a shepherd than to see well fed, frisky lambs playing on a warm spring evening.

Towards the end of April it is the turn of the cattle to be put out into the pastures. The long winter is over, and the cows and calves show their delight by racing round the fields before settling down to graze the fresh spring grass.

It is a satisfying time for the stockman. The long hours spent during the winter feeding, bedding and carefully tending the stock have been rewarded with healthy, well grown calves. The herd is grazed in separate groups which are made up of cows and calves of the same breeding pattern, an important factor in the efficient management control of both grassland and stock. Once the cattle have been turned out, the next job is to clean out the sheds and to wash down the concrete yards.

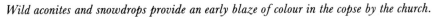

Wild aconites and snowdrops provide an early blaze of colour in the copse by the church.

*Opposite: A shaft of sunlight warms the woodland; the mist
rises and spiders' webs glisten.*

*Below: A robin establishes his breeding territory early, and will defend his patch vigorously by chasing off intruding robins and other
species of small birds which may challenge him.*

A long-eared owl perches close to the trunk of a larch tree, its sharp talons gripping the branch. A number of these handsome birds often spend the latter half of the winter with us. They are possibly migrants from Scandinavia.

Gulls hang on the wind before alighting onto the freshly turned soil to plunder the earthworms exposed by the plough.

The stockman and his assistant help to deliver a calf safely.

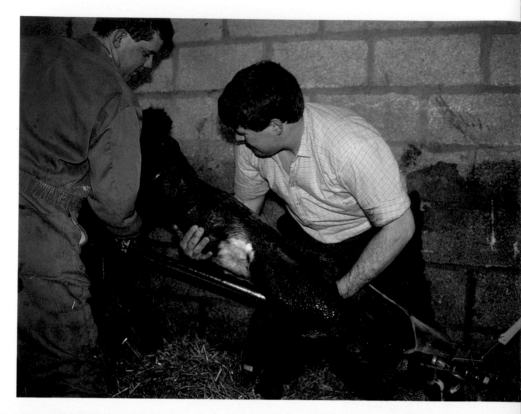

A fieldmouse emerges from his snug nest concealed under the moss. He has to watch out because his species forms a major part of the diet of our owls and kestrels.

The shining face of a celandine shows its intricate structure to the sun.

Dew drops on wild honeysuckle leaves are slowly evaporated by the gentle warmth of the sun.

41

Primroses are a true sign that spring is almost with us. They prefer to grow facing the sun on sheltered banks in the woodland and by the streams.

Early flowering coltsfoot adds a splash of colour to the banks of one of the ponds.

Below right: A young leveret hides behind a clump of winter barley. It is incredible how these tiny creatures survive the cold, driving rains which sweep across the fields during March.

Hazel catkins after a light snowfall.

A ewe with her new-born lambs.

Towards the end of March thousands of frogs arrive to mate and spawn in the ponds. The development of the aquatic ecology of a newly made pond is fascinating, and the creation of a new environment has a significant impact on the wildlife which inhabits the surrounding area.

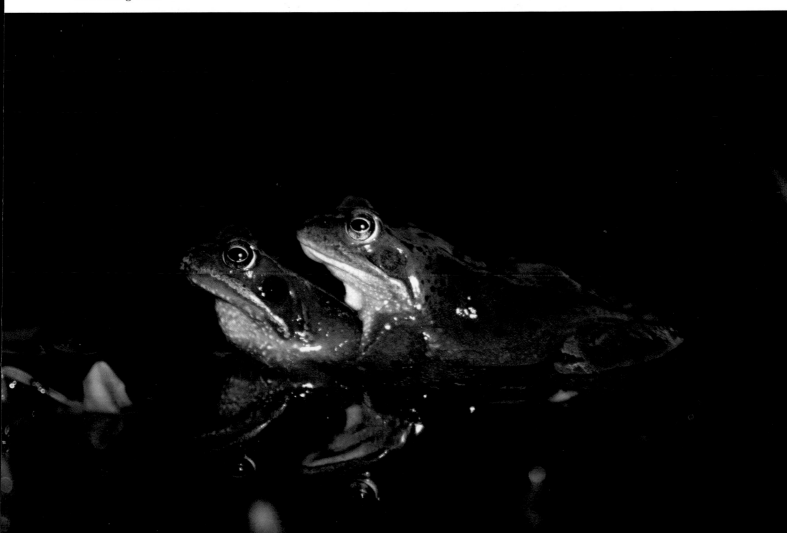

Opposite: Alder trees grow by the stream and the drooping catkins develop before the leaves come out.

Newly hatched song thrush chicks strike a remarkable contrast with the blue eggs.

Opposite: Pussy willow grows in damp places and flowers before the leaves develop.

A branch of a horse-chestnut tree overhangs the water and highlights the fresh unfurling leaves.

A mallard incubates her eggs in the safety of undergrowth in a wood some way from a pond.

Opposite: Giant horse-tails emerge from boggy areas by the streams and soon release their spores. Supported by bushes, they grow up to eight feet high.

In the spring while waiting for a badger to emerge from his sett at dusk, the sounds of the wild creatures break the still of the evening. The rich chorus of birdsong slowly fades and is replaced by the sounds of a drumming snipe and a roding woodcock. Overhead the whistling wings of a pair of mallard are accompanied by the loud quacking of the female. In the undergrowth woodmice rustle in the leaves and a hedgehog goes snuffling by. Suddenly, without warning and silently, the badger appears, his white facial stripes conspicuous in the gloom. He sniffs the air several times before completely emerging from his large oval hole. After having a good scratch he trundles off down one of his well worn tracks to the stream for a drink.

These larch flowers will soon grow into cones.

A tawny owl brings a shrew for her brood of chicks which occupy a snug nest in thick ivy clinging to a hawthorn tree. Photographing birds from a hide in April can be a chilly business, especially when the north-east wind blows showers of sleet across a grey sky at dawn or dusk.

Opposite: The delicate flowers of stitchwort growing in a woodland glade.

A handsome cock pheasant in full breeding plumage displays his ear tufts and bright red wattles.

SUMMER

May signals a turning point in the year as the mood of the countryside changes. The livestock which have been housed all winter now graze the lush pastures. The landscape, dominated for so long by the bare branches of the trees, turns to many shades of green when the buds burst into life and the woodland rings with birdsong as nesting territories are urgently established. May is a busy month on the farm too. The men go about their work with a fresh feeling of purpose: the longer days and the rapidly changing landscape herald a new beginning.

The stockman is aware of potential problems, so the herds of cows and calves have to be seen first thing in the morning and again each evening. He is looking for sick animals which may need his attention. He is also checking for cows in heat because May is one of the months when some of the pedigree Charolais cows are artificially inseminated with semen from bulls of new blood lines. The cows are in heat for only twenty-four hours every three weeks, and the inseminator has to call within that time if he is to get them in calf.

The shepherd also tends the three flocks of ewes and lambs twice a day. The ewes sometimes develop mastitis which must be treated quickly with antibiotics. Another hazardous situation is when they roll over onto their backs and, surprisingly perhaps, cannot right themselves because of their heavy fleeces. In this state they would die within a few hours.

Looking after the 2500 head of stock which range over 350 acres is a time-consuming job which is never finished, but each man approaches his task with an experienced eye and a dedication which ensures that the flocks and the herds are healthy and productive.

This male greater spotted woodpecker has just fed one of his chicks. Through the hours of daylight the young birds continually cheep, the pitch rising as a parent bird approaches with food.

During the first half of the month all the cattle and sheep sheds have to be cleaned out. For about ten days the farmyard manure is loaded into trailers and carted to a huge heap on the edge of a field. About 600 tonnes of this natural fertiliser is produced during the winter; it is allowed to rot down before being spread on the land to improve the fertility and humus content of the soil. As soon as the manure carting is complete the yards are pressure-washed and a general 'spring clean' smartens up the farmyard.

Thoughts then turn to silage making. This is a very busy time, involving six tractors working thirteen hours a day for six or seven days, cutting, carting and ensiling nearly 1000 tonnes of grass from 120 acres. Silage is a very important feed for the cattle in winter, and to achieve the high quality that is required for good animal performance it has to be made well. The most important factor in achieving this is to cut the grass when its feeding value is at its best, just before it starts to head, which is usually about the eighteenth of the month.

The main problem which inhibits making good silage is excess water interfering with the natural chemical reactions in the clamp, so a dry, settled period of weather is important for these few critical days. The grass is cut with a mower which leaves it in even swathes to dry out for twenty-four hours before the forage harvester picks it up, chops it into small pieces and then blows it into trailers. When the loads arrive back at the farm they are tipped up near the clamp, and the grass is then picked up by a big grab on a tractor and carted into the clamp where it is levelled out and rolled down by the tractor to squeeze the air out. Once all the grass is in the clamp it is covered with a plastic sheet which is weighted down with old tyres, to keep out the rain. As soon as all the grass is off the fields they are fertilised with nitrates and potash to ensure a good second crop in about a month's time.

All this hectic activity leaves me very little free time to photograph the rapidly changing wildlife scene. Dawn often finds me in a hide with my camera trained on a nesting bird, or by a pond trying to catch the early morning light playing on a freshly opened flower. Then all too soon time is up and I have to get back to work.

At the end of May, however, the work-load suddenly eases; I can have a break and leave the farm in the capable hands of my foreman. Usually I take my family and my camera to a remote part of North Wales, or to one of Scotland's many islands, to study and photograph the wildlife that inhabits those beautiful places.

By June the bright yellow petals of the oil seed rape plants have nearly all fallen. With luck the wild bees will have been busy pollinating the flowers to establish the pods that will carry the seeds of the crop to be harvested in early August. The winter barley crops are now a glorious sight as the wind races over the fields, swaying the tall plants in rippling waves of dancing ears. The deep green winter wheat's leaves have to be kept free from damaging fungal diseases with the careful use of fungicide sprays.

The suckling calves and lambs are growing apace on their mothers' milk. It is essential to ensure that the cows and ewes have enough grass, not only to maintain themselves but also to produce adequate milk for their offspring, so managing a grazing system is a delicate balancing act between the supply of grass and the demands of the livestock. The supply part of the equation involves encouraging the growth of the grass while on the other hand ensuring that stocking rates are at an adequate level to make full use of the grass produced. To encourage sufficient growth of grass to support our livestock population, regular applications of nitrogen fertiliser are spread on the pastures. The second of these is carried out early in the month using our four-wheel drive tractor. This has to be done with care on the steep slopes but the risk of accidents is reduced by fitting extra wheels onto the tractor.

Breeding better cattle is something that I am continually striving to achieve, but it is naturally a slow process because each cow has an average of only eight calves in her lifetime. Therefore, the rate of genetic improvement within a herd is limited, and so we use modern technology to multiply the best Charolais breeding lines at a faster rate than would naturally occur. Cows which produce offspring exhibiting superior performance and breed characteristics are used in an embryo-transfer programme. These donor cows are superovulated and then inseminated with semen from selected bulls. Seven days later a specialist team of vets flush the fertilised ova out of the donors and implant them in the wombs of recipient cross-bred cows. This highly skilled technique enables the cross-bred cows to give birth to and rear valuable pedigree calves, which enter the herd, and at the same time accelerate the genetic improvement of the herd.

It will soon be warm enough to relieve the ewes of their heavy fleeces. This is a busy time for the shepherd; he has to gather the flocks early in the mornings to be ready for the three contract shearers to start work at 7.00 am. He catches 300 sheep for them each day and he works his dogs to move the flocks in and out of the shearing sheds at the right times.

As soon as the fleeces have been taken off they are wrapped and put into big nylon bags which are delivered to the local wool marketing centre, where they are graded before distribution.

When shearing has finished the shepherd takes a well-earned holiday. This usually coincides with the stockman's holiday and while they are away I check the cattle and sheep daily and deal with any problems which may arise. I enjoy this period because I can spend more time with the stock than usual, and driving around the grass-land gives me extra opportunities to observe the changing wildlife scene. Many of my photographs are taken at opportune moments so I am always on the look-out for subjects that will make interesting pictures.

Meanwhile the arable farming staff walk the winter barley fields to 'rogue' by hand any stray wild oats or sterile brome plants. These grass weeds must be taken out of the crops because most of our barley is sold as seed, and it would be rejected by the inspectors if found to be contaminated by unwanted seeds.

By the middle of the month I watch the weather forecasts more closely than usual because I am hoping for a few hot days to make some hay. We cut ten acres of grass each year which provides the shepherd with about twenty tonnes of hay to feed the ewes during the lambing period.

Time passes quickly, and before we know where we are the silage grass is ready to be cut once again. The second cut is not as heavy as the first and therefore does not take as long to complete. By the time we have finished the clamp is full, and we are assured of sufficient silage to see the cattle through the next winter.

The corn fields slowly change from shades of green to rich golden-brown as the grains fill and then ripen. We have done all we can to ensure that the crops achieve their full potential yield. They have been sown into properly prepared seed beds and kept free from competing weeds. They have been fertilised and protected from numerous pests and diseases. Now it is up to Mother Nature to complete our work: we watch and wait as the long sunny days pass, drawing harvest time ever closer.

July is a relatively quiet month on the farm. The rush of all the spring work is behind us and before us lie hectic weeks of harvesting, autumn cultivations and planting next year's crops. It is a good time for the men to go on their holidays. Of course, they cannot all go at once because there are always jobs to be done around the farm, so they stagger their holidays, leaving at least three of us behind on the farm.

One important job which has to be done early in the month is sheep dipping, the purpose of which is to kill parasites living in the wool and on the skin of the sheep. Dipping also prevents fly strike, a particularly nasty condition where flies lay their eggs near the tail of the sheep. The eggs hatch and the maggots feed on the flesh of the unfortunate animal.

An early start is necessary for us to dip all the sheep in a day. The shepherd has already filled the swim-through dip with 1000 gallons of clean water. He has also gathered all the flocks so they are handy. The dip concentrate is added to the water and away they go, swimming through the wash.

Some Agricultural Societies take advantage of the lull in the work-load on farms and hold their annual shows in July. I usually have a day at the Royal Show and the Great Yorkshire Show. I find these days rewarding because the exhibits of machinery and technology keep me in touch with new developments, and I can see some of the best of British cattle. The shows are also meeting places for old friends and new acquaintances.

I 1987 I attended the Great Yorkshire Show for a special reason. I had entered the farm in the Yorkshire Agricultural Society's Farm Competition. After the judging had taken place I was informed that Givendale had been placed first in the class for 500 acres or more, and I was requested to attend a presentation ceremony in the main ring where the overall championship would be announced. After all the class winners had received their trophies we waited in hushed anticipation for the champion to be declared. To my surprise, I was called up to receive the award. It was a proud moment for me and I was pleased for the farm staff whose expertise and dedication contributed to the high standards of husbandry required to win inter-farm competitions.

Ever mindful that the corn harvest will soon be upon us, preparation work forges ahead. There are many measures that we can take to minimise time-wasting breakdowns. For instance, thorough maintenance of the harvesting and corn-drying machinery is time well spent. Less obvious things like having spare wheels for the tractors and trailers can save valuable time when punctures occur, and we also have a stock of various spare parts to keep machinery going with the minimum of delay.

Just before harvest starts in August we wean the ten-month-old calves that have been suckling their mothers out in the pastures. This is a time of intense interest for the stockman because the weight and number of calves weaned directly reflects how well he has managed the herd all year. When the calves are taken away from their mothers they are wormed and weighed, and are then housed for a few months before being sold as beef. The cows are dried off and rested before they start a new cycle by calving in six weeks' time.

The bare ash trees stand out in contrast to the maples which are dusted with a pale green haze as their buds burst. In the larch wood on the far side of the valley there is a hive of activity as song birds feed their first broods and a pair of sparrow-hawks secretly build their nest high in a tree. A lone sycamore, now in full leaf, stands at the end of a field of oil seed rape in brilliant flower, shining like an extra sun on the hillside, and the cattle are contented in the valley.

I found this long-eared bat hanging outside a hole in the trunk of a hollow ash tree, and managed to photograph it before it took off for its evening feed.

Common blue butterflies now breed in our roadside verges. My policy of mowing these areas only once a year in the winter has encouraged wild flowers to flourish, resulting in an increase in the number of species of butterflies.

Opposite: Ferns uncurling their long fronds under the open canopy of an ash woodland.

Picking up mown grass to be carted back to the silage clamp. In the distance the Vale of York stretches away towards the Pennines.

Opposite: Bluebells abound in glades between the ash trees where mature woodland borders the meadows.

Below: I got to know this comical young tawny owl quite well. He had the habit of falling out of the nest, and fearful that something untoward might happen to him, I carried him back up the tree several times. He became quite used to my helping hand, and poses here for our last encounter.

Fly honeysuckle. This rare shrub grows in several woods on the farm, its tiny flowers inconspicuous in the shade.

Several magnificent crab apple trees growing on the farm add to the kaleidoscope of spring colours.

An early nester — this long-tailed tit has built its intricate nest protected by the sharp thorns of a wild rose. Unfortunately, many early nests of song birds are destroyed by marauding magpies and jays. This was the only one of six nests I found that successfully fledged.

Opposite: The delicate flowers of baneberry growing in undisturbed woodland.

This inquisitive fox cub pops its head out from under an old wood pile, to which the vixen had moved her litter after being disturbed at her nursery earth.

Opposite: The handsome orange tip is one of the first butterflies to be seen in the spring flying down woodland margins.

A moorhen sits tight on her eggs close to the edge of a pond.

Opposite: Graceful water avens grow in abundance along the banks of the streams.

Below: A beautiful peacock butterfly feeds on the nectar of oil seed rape. A high level of insect activity pollinates the bright flowers to set the pods for a good crop.

The farm ponds are fed by pure spring water so they are rich in plant and animal life, supporting birds such as this dab-chick. She incubates her eggs on a floating platform of water weed anchored to a fallen branch in the shallow water.

Thick banks of yellow flag break the water's edge and provide cover for birds and many insects.

Dappled light penetrating the canopy plays on these new sycamore leaves.

A robin approaches its hungry brood.

'Starburst'.

A cow suckles her calf.

After a long incubation the first kestrel chick pops its head out from under the soft feathers of its mother's breast.

Opposite: Ripening sycamore seeds.

A red-legged partridge incubates her eggs in the safety of a hedge bottom.

Poppies sometimes embarrass farmers by turning whole fields blood red after they have got their spraying programmes wrong, but this one was growing out of the side of our silage clamp.

The furry bonnets of the white deadnettle — a very common plant of hedgerows but one which deserves a closer look.

Opposite: A tree creeper carries insects to feed its growing brood hidden behind the rotten wood of this ash tree.

The bright beaks of these dunnock chicks exhibit a good guidance system for their feeding parents to home in on.

Opposite: Several pairs of spotted flycatchers nest on the farm. They use their agile, flickering flight to ambush passing insects from favourite perches such as fencing posts.

Below: Clustered bell flowers add to the variety of flowers growing in the chalky soils along track sides and woodland margins.

A young roe fawn lies under the shade of a small beech tree. The doe will be back to feed it at dusk.

The male kestrel feeds his hungry brood with torn pieces of vole.

The female kestrel alights just above her nest, a short-tailed vole gripped tightly in her beak.

A hungry brood of jay chicks beg for food as a parent bird prepares to regurgitate their next meal into their gaping, crimson beaks.

A little owl stands guard outside its nesting site.

Above: At dusk, the female jay settles down to keep her chicks warm for the night.

Below: A group of Pleurotus Pulmonarius *graces the ivy-covered stump of an old tree.*

The shepherd rounds up a flock of ewes and lambs in readiness for dipping.

At the end of the month the calves are weaned. This one weighed just five kilos less than his mother and he was only ten months old!

This snail wraps itself round a slender giant horse-tail.

A tender moment for a female sparrow-hawk as her chicks pay close attention to her arrival. This was the first nest I photographed, and I will never forget my excitement at witnessing the family life of these wild birds from only a few feet away.

Opposite: A pair of green-veined whites mate before the female lays her eggs on hedge or garlic mustard.

A ringlet butterfly feeding on cow parsley growing at the edge of a field of wheat.

Opposite: A magnificent spotted orchid. They grow in several damp places on the farm.

These young little owls wait for another meal. In a few days they will fly with their parents to be taught how to catch earthworms and night flying beetles.

Dog roses grow in abundance in the thick hedges and on the woodland margins.

The sinister flowers of deadly nightshade, their curved stamens beckoning menacingly.

*Dryad's saddle growing out of a rotten tree stump, photographed
here after a shower.*

A beautiful elephant hawk-moth is attracted to wild
honeysuckle. The banks of willowherb on the farm play host
to its caterpillars.

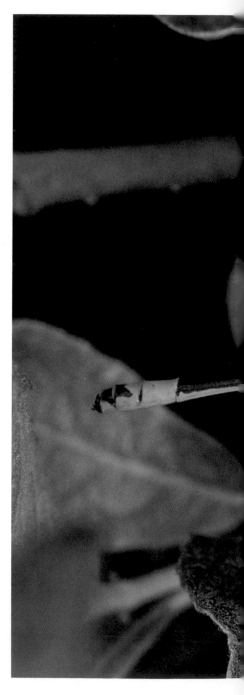

A blue damselfly tucking into its prey. These brilliant insects breed in the ponds and can be seen hovering over the water during the summer.

Early one morning I walked down to the spinney where I had built a hide to photograph a sparrow-hawk's nest. There had been a shower overnight and as I crept through the undergrowth the trees dripped all around me in the still, dank atmosphere. I climbed up the slippery hawthorn tree to my hide and settled down on the wet plank, my camera trained at the nest. Only nine feet away the three young hawks slept in a huddled heap in the middle of their flat platform. As I waited, the woodland started to come to life again after my intrusion. Birdsong soon filled the air and a pair of courting wood-pigeons played chase in a nearby ash tree, stopping now and then to bill and coo to each other.

Suddenly I heard a wing flap, and there was a flash in the corner of my eye. I hardly dared move a muscle; the female hawk had landed about twenty feet away. She called softly to her chicks, they looked up at her, re-arranged themselves and then went back to sleep. She settled down to wait for her mate to bring the next meal for their brood. I kept perfectly still as I indulged myself in the privilege of being so close to the wild hunter. She sat, hunched and motionless, one eye half open watching the surrounding area. Through my peephole I spotted the looping flight of a family of long-tailed tits coming towards us; they passed by calling to each other unaware of the potential danger. Her cold eye followed them but she remained motionless.

Then the sound of cracking twigs echoed through the trees. The hawk sat bolt upright, her fierce yellow eyes glaring down at the woodland floor. She soon relaxed again and I wondered what creature was down there to have caused such consternation. I parted a corner of my hessian hide very carefully and there a roe buck stood, his red summer coat shining in a shaft of early morning sunlight. A few moments later, I heard the male hawk calling away in the trees, she immediately answered him and left her perch to collect the prey he had caught. The chicks had also heard the call and they showed excitement at the prospect of a good breakfast. She quickly returned to the nest clutching a plucked corpse in her powerful talons. Tearing at it with her hooked beak, she rapidly fed her chicks one by one and then flipped off the nest to disappear through the trees carrying with her the boney remains of the corpse. It was time for me to leave the fascinating world of the wild creatures and return to the reality of farming.

A puss moth caterpillar gnaws its way down the stem of a poplar leaf.

106

Behind an inquisitive group of Charolais cows and calves the hills roll away up to the skyline. On the distant, steep, grassy slopes other groups of cattle graze and the fields of winter barley turn a golden brown as the straw dies and the grain ripens.

AUTUMN

Harvesting is a very busy and an immensely satisfying part of the farming year, but I always approach it with some apprehension because our unpredictable climate can cause terrible damage to the crops that we have nurtured for so long. Unsettled weather also causes us extra and frustrating work, which adds to the cost of drying the corn and turning wet straw before it can be baled. But whatever the weather the job must go on because during the next few weeks the profit from the arable crops is either lost or won. Nearly 1500 tonnes of grain are harvested by the combine and carted back to the yard to be dried and stored. The first crop to ripen is the winter barley, closely followed by the oil seed rape. I make the decision to start combining when the moisture content of the grain is low enough to suit the conditions. If the weather is good then I may wait until the moisture content drops to about 16 per cent but if the weather is unsettled and the grain is being damaged then I will combine it nearer to 20 per cent.

Every day the combine starts up as soon as the early morning dew evaporates and it keeps going right through the day until after sunset, when the dew returns and stops the straw from going through the machine properly. It moves steadily across the fields leaving tidy swathes of straw in a cloud of dust which is quickly dispersed by the drying winds.

Each time the grain tank on the combine is filled, the huge unloading auger swings out to empty the corn into the trailers running along-side. Back in the yard the moisture content of each six-tonne load is checked and recorded before the elevator carries the grain into the store.

Following behind the combine, our baler wraps the straw into big round bales which are

Opposite: The neat rows of straw are wrapped into round bales, soon to be carted and stacked near the livestock sheds.

used to feed and bed the cattle and sheep during the coming winter. A total of 2000 bales are made and they are carted and stacked close to the stock sheds. When the fields have been cleared our big four-wheel drive tractor goes in to plough them in readiness for the next crops to be planted.

Meanwhile the cattle and sheep still demand daily attention. During the first half of the month the shepherd weans the lambs because the milk supply from the ewes starts to diminish as the feeding value of the grass deteriorates. At this stage the lambs are taken away from their mothers and moved into the fields which have grown good quality grass after being cut for silage making. Before the lambs are moved into the fresh pastures they are wormed and vaccinated to prevent illness and deaths from parasitic and clostridial diseases. They soon put on weight grazing the nutritious grass and by the end of the month the heaviest ones are sold to the abattoir.

The calves born earlier in the year are still suckling their mothers, but because the nutritional value of the permanent grass is declining they, like the lambs, need extra feed, to maintain good growth rates. So self-feed hoppers, which only the calves can get into, are put out into the fields. A daily ration of cereal mix is then fed to the calves; as they grow bigger so the ration is increased.

By the end of August, if the weather has been kind to us, we will be half-way through the autumn campaign. Three-quarters of the harvest is complete and next year's oil seed rape crop has already been sown; the rows of tiny plants are just visible.

A great deal of work is behind us but we are still combining winter wheat, and the next four weeks or so will be equally hectic.

We approach the remaining harvest work with increased urgency, because the days are growing noticeably shorter and there is a distinct feel of autumn in the air. In still weather the morning dews are heavier and the wheat takes longer to dry out, delaying the start of combining. To compensate, on windy days we keep the combine running well into the night. The blazing lights of the huge machine pierce the dust-filled air as the driver sits at the controls in his air-conditioned cab, his attention focussed on the cutter bar and the whirling pick-up reel below him.

There is always a great sense of relief among the men as the last run of wheat is cut and the final load arrives back at the grain store. The first stage of the autumn campaign is done, but the men know that the pressure is still on because the target is to have nearly 400 acres re-sown by the end of the month.

All around, the golden fields of stubble are dotted with hundreds of bales, but they are soon cleared and the fields take on a different hue as the plough buries the stubble, exposing the dark soil. As the big four-wheel drive tractor ploughs on it is often followed by a squawking stream of hungry gulls eagerly pouncing on the earthworms in the freshly turned soil. Behind the plough, tractors pull machines preparing the level, firm seed beds into which next year's crops are soon to be sown. Heavy rollers follow the drill, pressing the seed into close contact with the soil so ensuring even germination to establish the new crop.

The team forge relentlessly on, starting early and often working into the night, always aware that the weather might break at any time. On the wet days most of the action comes to a halt and there is time to catch up on some of the jobs that we haven't recently had time to do. There are machines to repair, spare parts to collect, tractors to service and when the last of the corn is cut, the combine is cleaned down and put away.

I must leave the farm for a day when the breeding sheep sale is held at Bellingham in Northumberland. I make an early start with the shepherd and we drive north through Yorkshire and the rolling hills of Durham. Eventually we stop for breakfast on wild moorland above Bellingham. Before us lies a spectacular view. In the foreground, suckler cows and blackface sheep graze the coarse hill grasses and in the distance

the massive Kielder Forest stretches away as far as the eye can see. In the valley below the small market town prepares for a busy day. Farmers from miles around are bringing their lambs to the mart, filling the wooden pens with groups of about twenty animals. These proud stockmen will have spent many hours drawing their sheep in even groups and dressing the fleeces to smarten them up.

Sheep farming is the life-blood of these upland areas and many thousands of ewe lambs are reared to be sold to lowland flockmasters as breeding stock. These hardy sheep are very prolific and they have strong mothering instincts, developed by surviving in the hills. Each year I buy about 200 of them as replacements for our flock. When we arrive in the mart, local farmers whom we have got to know over the years are pleased to see us and they are keen to show us their consignments. If we like them we mark the pen numbers in the catalogue for possible purchase later in the auction. By about 2.30 pm all 7000 lambs will have been sold and it is time to load ours into the lorry which has come up from Yorkshire. As I drive up the hill out of the town, I can't help but admire the men who present such superb stock from this dramatic but harsh environment. They are men who, against the odds, survive on the poorest land, in a hostile climate, but to help them they enjoy a kind of comradeship unknown in any other walk of life.

Back home, the suckler herd starts to calve in the middle of the month. A few days before the cows are due we move them into a field close to the farm buildings so that the stockman can keep a close watch over them. Meanwhile the arable team presses on sowing field after field. Finally the machines pull out of the last one, their work done for another season.

By October the new crops of wheat and barley are already peeping through, but also growing amongst them are weed seedlings, which must be controlled to prevent them competing with the crops. This is done by spraying the fields with selective herbicides through a tractor-mounted machine, but only on calm days to avoid the spray drifting away from the target areas. Of course, the safe use of farm chemicals is essential, so today's operators are highly trained and they have to pass strict proficiency tests before being allowed to use spraying equipment. In addition there are safeguards governing the handling of chemicals, including the correct methods of disposing of empty containers. These measures are designed to ensure the correct use of all agricultural chemicals but we rely completely on manufacturers to suppy us with well tested materials to perform their designed roles effectively, economically and as safely as possible.

Calving is now in full swing, so the herd demands twenty-four hour attention. The stockman bears the brunt of the work but I am on hand to help out and to do the late night shift. Waiting up for cows to calve night after night can be very exhausting; there is no time to catch up on sleep during the day. So we have developed a routine which is intended to achieve the best possible results but which also makes life tolerable. The cows are seen every three hours around the clock, the two night shifts being shared between the stockman and myself. After doing the evening check at about 8.30 pm I drive down to the calving field in the Land-Rover at about midnight. The searchlight is already plugged into the vehicle's electrical system so I just switch it on and sweep the powerful beam over the field picking up the cows, most of which will be lying down cudding. I am looking for those cows which have either recently calved or those showing signs of imminent calving. A systematic search of the field might find one with her back arched and tail held straight out, and then I know I am in for a wait because I cannot go to bed until the calf has been born. If, after a while, I decide that she needs help I will drive her into the special catching pen to calve her.

Whilst on these night-time patrols I often pick up nocturnal feeders in the beam of the searchlight. The piercing eyes of foxes flash in the distance as they quarter the calving field looking for afterbirths to feed on. A solitary woodcock may quickly rise out of a damp hollow where its long bill will have been probing the soft turf for a worm or two. A little owl often perches in its favourite oak tree waiting to pounce on a passing beetle while bats hunt for insects in the night sky. Occasionally, a ghostly barn owl drifts over the field on long elegant wings, hovering now and then above the slightest rustle in the thick grass before dropping like a stone, talons outstretched. I enjoy these sightings; they are not only a bonus on tiring nights but they also help to reassure me that our farming system is still a rich and well balanced one, since it supports such a variety of predators at the end of the food chain.

My midnight visit to the calving field is followed at about 3.00 am by the stockman who carries out the same routine. In the morning, the new calves are ear-tagged to correspond with their mothers' numbers and they are turned out of the calving field. The long hours tending the herd are well rewarded when one sees the fit, young calves race around the fields on a warm autumn evening, their mothers looking anxiously on.

The autumn livestock sales are in full swing at the local markets. Cattle and sheep of all types fill the pens and the selling rings are crowded with farmers bidding for those lots which take their fancy. One of these days is the special autumn show and sale, when pens of cattle are judged and the best of them awarded prizes. I take our suckled heifer calves to this sale, but before they leave the farm we trim the long hair off to smarten them up and to show off their good conformation. Farmers like to buy our type of quality cattle which will sell for beef at a good price after they have finished them. I am always a little apprehensive before they are sold but when they make good prices I am delighted; it is a just reward for all the effort that has gone into producing them over the past year.

A male barn owl drops in with a young rat to feed his incubating mate.

Evening sun highlights a cloud of dust following the combine up a hill, as wheat is tipped into a trailer running alongside.

This juvenile female sparrow-hawk already exhibits a fearsome appearance.

113

A spectacular study of orange hawkweed ('fox and cubs').

A poplar hawk-moth. Caterpillars of this handsome moth feed on the leaves of willow and poplar trees growing on the farm.

A treasured colony of marbled white butterflies has recently established itself on the farm.

Opposite: A scalloped oak moth at rest.

The lacewing is not only beneficial, feeding on greenfly, but it is also a beautiful insect.

Opposite: Graceful meadow sweet adds to the variety of marsh plants growing in damp places.

The garden tiger moth looks an awesome beast in this close-up study.

Big bales of straw cast shadows across the stubble.

The seed-head of goat's beard interwoven like a spider's web.

Below: Young wood-pigeons help themselves to a meal from their mother's crop. The soft cooing of these gentle birds adds a richness to the variety of woodland sounds in the spring and summer, but when they flock in the winter they can cause severe damage to farmers' crops.

A calf, just an hour or so old, wobbles on unsteady legs as it looks for its first feed of colostrum.

One of the sycamore trees which grace the pastures casting shadows in the early morning.

124

Mule ewe lambs arriving at Bellingham Mart.

This garden spider spins a web around a common harvester before devouring it.

127

Opposite: Mist rises off the water as the first rays of sun warm the chill air of dawn, and evaporate the dew drops hanging on the downy seeds of the willow herb.

Young barn owls with down still clinging to their new feathers venture out of their nest for the first time. At dusk, for about a week they climb up from deep inside the hollow elm tree, hissing loudly as they appear at the entrance hole. They stretch and flap their wings and each evening become more adventurous as they half-jump and half-fly from branch to branch. At last, with a backward glance, they fly off into the night to learn how to fend for themselves.

Opposite: The brilliant bunches of guelder rose berries grace the stream sides.

A nocturnal rambler hunts for earthworms in the damp grass. The hedgehog feeds well in the autumn, building up fat reserves to sustain it through the long winter hibernation.

A young roe buck stands alert in a woodland glade.

Pleurotus Cornucopiae *forms an interesting family group as it grows on an old tree stump which has been left to rot in woodland.*

A group of shaggy pholiota growing from the base of a horse-chestnut tree.

The yellow tag identifies this well-nourished calf with its mother. They will stay together for ten months, the calf growing rapidly on a plentiful supply of milk.

A group of cows and calves enjoying a bright, warm autumn day. In the next field, a new crop of winter barley is already through. Early establishment is essential at this altitude to ensure the crop survives the frosts and cold winds of winter.

Opposite: The brilliant poisonous fruits of lords and ladies growing in the woodland.

Overleaf: The pastel shades of a dawn sky are reflected by the still water on this misty autumn morning.

Five species of tits occur on the farm, breeding in the deciduous woodland. This blue tit visits my garden and is framed in a cotoneaster bush.

Givendale Valley — the golden leaves of autumn fall as the sun sweeps low in the sky, casting long shadows across the fields.

REFLECTIONS

It gives me great pleasure to stroll around the farm on a calm, sunny afternoon and look with satisfaction at next year's crops growing in neat, green rows stretching away up the fields. The machinery that spent so many hours roaring over the land is now at rest, and there is time to reflect on the successes and failures of the past year. There is also time to appreciate living and working in these wonderful surroundings, something one can easily forget to do when the pressure is on, with dozens of jobs all crying out to be done at once.

As I wander on, the golden leaves of autumn are starting to fall; the first frosts have weakened their hold on the branches and the slightest breeze sends them spinning to the ground. A carpet of dead leaves lies under the trees until the next storm will blow them into heaps against a fence or into a corner of the farmyard. Damp tree trunks steam in the gentle warmth of the hazy sun as it sweeps low in the sky, casting long shadows across the fields. I notice the badgers have already reinstated their traditional track meandering across the rows of wheat; and on the edge of a field, in the soft earth, two sets of roe deer slots, one larger than the other, confirm that the doe still runs with her fawn. Down by a stream in a larch wood, a mixed flock of tits moves through the branches, the birds calling to each other as they hunt for morsels.

Suddenly a marauding sparrow-hawk flashes through the trees, sending the tits scattering for cover with a flurry of alarm calls. He bursts out of the wood, his blue wings shining in the sunlight, and dashes away down a hedge hoping to surprise a solitary bird.

As I make for home in the rich evening light, the redwings and fieldfares scramble in the hawthorn bushes, filling their crops with the dark red berries to give them energy to survive the on-coming chill of the night. Silhouetted against the setting sun, a kestrel hovers over a patch of rough grass hoping to catch a short-tailed vole unawares. As darkness falls, the tawny owls down the valley start hooting to each other and a rush of wings heralds the arrival of a flight of mallard at the ponds.

When I reach the head of the valley, I turn to marvel at the reflection of the moon on the water where the black shapes of the feeding ducks are encircled by rings of silver ripples. To my surprise, I spot a long-eared bat on what must be his last outing before hibernating, his crazy flight difficult to follow in the shadows. l linger, soaking up the atmosphere and I reflect on my afternoon's stroll through beautiful countryside observing the well-being of the wild life and the promising crops. I turn and pick my way through the spinney at the bottom of my garden; a roosting cock pheasant startles me as he clatters out of the holly tree.

As I pull my boots off at the back door I feel a deep sense of contentment from knowing that some of my actions in the past have helped to create this rich environment in which I am privileged to live and work, but of which I am only the temporary custodian.

The first hard frost of winter decorates a spear thistle.

APPENDIX

My first camera was a Kodak Brownie which I used to record interesting events. I can remember being excited when I managed to take some pleasing shots of a grey squirrel by a roadside. In my late teens I graduated to an Ilford Sportsman which served me well for many years. I used it to photograph our family growing up, and various farming activities. I managed to photograph the odd flower and fungus, but I didn't seem to have the time or the money to take photography very seriously. It wasn't until 1984 when I needed some good shots of Givendale and of the cattle that I really started to take a keen interest in it. It was obvious that I had to buy a new camera but the world of SLRs and interchangeable lenses was a complete mystery to me, so I took advice from a colleague and consequently I bought a fairly cheap camera complete with a 50mm and a 70–200mm zoom lens.

After a period of taking shots on a trial and error basis my results eventually improved and encouraged by this, I started to take a much keener interest in photography. It was while I was on holiday in the Lake District that I made a breakthrough in taking pictures of wildlife. My wife had persuaded me to take a weekend off after a particularly difficult harvest which had been prolonged by wet weather. We arrived in the Lake District to find yet more wet weather. Armed with my fairly new camera I was desperate to take photographs but the hills were shrouded in cloud, while grey, violent waterfalls rushed from out of the mist. However we braved the elements as we had done on the farm for most of that summer, and we went for walks in the rain. It was on one of these rambles, just before dusk, that we came across a superb group of fly agaric fungi which were growing under some silver birch trees. I took out my camera, fixed my free flash gun and fired away. When the transparencies came back I was over the moon. I had successfully found an exciting way of recording the wonders of my world.

Over the next year or so I worked away with my camera trying to improve the results. One day I was showing some of my slides to a friend and he suggested that I should enter some of my wildlife prints in an Arts Festival that was being held in the nearby town. In due course about a dozen of my prints were exhibited and on the strength of them, I was invited to give a slide show to the Arts Society. Nervously I presented my slides to a totally hushed audience and I thought to myself, 'Oh dear, this isn't going down too well'. It wasn't until afterwards that I learned that the audience had been spellbound.

My friend informed me that to do my photographs complete justice I had to buy a camera with better optics. He had a particular camera in mind but when he mentioned the price I backed off quickly. However, he was very persistent and eventually I succumbed to his pressure. I was photographing a sparrow-hawk feeding her chicks at the time, and I had built my hide only eight feet from the nest so the bird could hear my camera's shutter going off and me winding the film on.

The camera that I was taken to buy appealed to me because it had auto-focus and auto-wind facilities which would obviously make hide work easier. I sent my first reel of film off to be developed, and when the slides came back I was thrilled with them. I selected one of the sparrow-hawk and sent it off to a competition that was being run by the Game Fair and *The Yorkshire Post*. To my amazement it was chosen as runner-up to the winner. My prize money was immediately spent on another lens for my new camera.

This is how my photography developed, as I tried to record some of the wonderful secrets of the wildlife which surrounds me in this, my patch of the Yorkshire countryside. It has given great satisfaction to me and also evident pleasure to many others.

SPECIES LIST

A Aconite *(Eranthis hyemalis)*
Alder *(Alnus glutinosa)*

B Badger *(Meles meles)*
Baneberry *(Actaea spicata)*
Barn Owl *(Tyto alba)*
Black Bryony *(Tamus communis)*
Bluebell
    (Hyacinthoides non-scriptus)
Blue Tit *(Parus caeruleus)*
Bonnet Mycena
    (Mycena galericulata)
Brimstone *(Gonepteryx rhamni)*

C Celandine *(Ranunculus ficaria)*
Clustered Bell Flower
    (C. glomerata)
Coltsfoot *(Tussilago farfara)*
Common Blue
    (Polyommatus icarus)
Crab Apple *(Malus sylvestris)*

D Dab-chick *(Podiceps ruficollis)*
Deadly Nightshade
    (Atropa belladonna)
Dog Rose *(Rosa canina)*
Dryad's Saddle
    (Polyporus squamosus)
Dunnock *(Prunella modularis)*

E Elephant Hawk-moth
    (Deilephila elpenor)

F Ferns *(Polypodiaceae)*
Fly Honeysuckle
    (Lonicera xylosteum)
Fox *(Vulpes vulpes)*
Fox and Cubs
    (Hieracium aurantiacum)
Frog *(Rana temporaria)*

G Garden Spider
    (Araneus diadematus)
Garden Tiger moth *(Arctia caja)*
Goat's Beard
    (Tragopogon pratensis)
Greater Spotted Woodpecker
    (Dendrocopos major)
Great Tit *(Parus major)*
Green-veined White *(Pieris napi)*

Green-woodpecker *(Picus viridis)*
Guelder Rose *(Viburnum opulus)*

H Harvestman *(Opiliones SP)*
Hawthorn *(Crataegus monogyna)*
Hazel *(Lorylus avellana)*
Hedgehog *(Erinaceus europaeus)*
Honeysuckle
    (Lonicera periclymenum)
Horse-chestnut
    (Aesculus hippocastanum)
Horse-tail *(Equisetum arvense)*

I *Imomotus radiatus*
    (no common name)

J Jay *(Garrulus glamdarius)*

K Kestrel *(Falco tinnunculus)*

L Lacewing *(Chrysopa SP)*
Larch *(Larix decidua)*
Leveret *(Lepus europaeus)*
Little Owl *(Athene noctua)*
Long-eared bat *(Plecotus auritus)*
Long-eared owl *(Asio otus)*
Long-tailed Tit
    (Aegithalos caudatus)
Lords and Ladies
    (Arum maculatum)

M Mallard *(Anas platyrhynchas)*
Marbled White butterfly
    (Melanargia galathea)
Marsh marigold *(Caltha palustris)*
Meadow sweet
    (Filipendula ulmaria)
Milk cap *(Lactarius deliciosus)*
Moorhen *(Gallinula chloropus)*

N Nettle *(Urtica dioica)*

O Orange tip
    (Anthocharis cardamines)

P Peacock *(Nymphalis io)*
Pheasant *(Phasianus colchicus)*
Pleurotus cornucopiae
    (no common name)

Pleurotus Pulmonarius
    (no common name)
Poplar (Aspen)
    (Populus tremula)
Poplar Hawk-moth
    (Laothoe populi)
Poppy *(Papaver rhoeas)*
Primrose *(Primula vulgaris)*
Puss Moth *(Cerua vinula)*
Pussy Willow *(Salix caprea)*

R Red-legged partridge
    (Alectoris rufa)
Ringlet butterfly
    (Aphantopus hyperantus)
Robin *(Erithacus rubecula)*
Roe deer *(Capreolus capreolus)*

S Scalloped Oak moth
    (Crocallis elinguaria)
Selfheal *(Prunella vulgaris)*
Shaggy pholiota
    (Pholiota squarrosa)
Snail *(Cepaea hortensis)*
Song thrush *(Turdus philomelos)*
Sparrow-hawk *(Accipiter nisus)*
Spear thistle *(Cirsium vulgare)*
Spotted Flycatcher
    (Muscicapa striata)
Spotted orchis
    (Dectylorhiza fuchsii)
Stitchwort *(Stellaria holostea)*
Sycamore *(A. pseudoplatamus)*

T Tawny Owl *(Strix aluco)*
Tree creeper *(Certhia familiaris)*

V Velvetshank *(Collybia velutipes)*

W Water Avens *(Geum rivale)*
White deadnettle
    (Lamium album)
Woodmouse
    (Apodemus sylvaticus)
Wood-pigeon
    (Columba palumbus)

Y Yellow flag *(Iris pseudacorus)*